MODERN BRITISH ART

DANNY PEARSON

Badger Publishing Limited
Oldmedow Road,
Hardwick Industrial Estate,
King's Lynn PE30 4JJ
Telephone: 01438 791037

www.badgerlearning.co.uk

2 4 6 8 10 9 7 5 3 1

Modern British Art ISBN 978-1-78147-545-4

Publisher: Susan Ross
Senior Editor: Danny Pearson
Designer: Fiona Grant

Photos: Cover Image: REX/The Travel Library
Page 4: KeystoneUSA/ZUMA/REX
Page 5: Sipa Press/REX
Page 7: Neale Clark/Robert Harding/REX
Page 9: Ray Tang/REX
Page 10: Design Pics Inc/REX
Page 11: REX
Page 12: Tony Kyriacou/REX
Page 13: Sipa Press/REX
Page 14: Tony Kyriacou/REX
Page 15: David Hockney
Page 16: Jon Bradley/REX
Page 17: Andy Paradise/REX
Page 18: Alex Segre/REX
Page 19: Nils Jorgensen/REX
Page 20: Ray Tang/REX
Page 21: Prudence Cuming/ScienceLtd/W/REX
Page 22: Polly Morgan/Vestige
Page 23: Polly Morgan/Receiver
Page 25: Nicholas Bailey/REX
Page 26: Banksy TV
Page 27: Julian Makey/REX
Page 28: Rozenn Leboucher/REX
Page 29: Photofusion/REX
Page 30: Richard Gardner/REX
Page 31: Ian Lamond/Alamy

Attempts to contact all copyright holders have been made.
If any omitted would care to contact Badger Learning, we will be happy to make appropriate arrangements.

Page 23: Please note, some parts have been reworded to a more suitable reading level.

MODERN BRITISH ART

Contents

1. WHAT IS ART?

Art can be a painting, a drawing, a sculpture, almost anything. It can hang on a wall in a famous art gallery or it can stand high on top of a hill.

It can be made by a famous artist and be worth millions of pounds. Or it can be made by a small child in a classroom using a pencil and paper.

Art is many things to many people. In comparison to the rest of the world, Great Britain is relatively small, but some of the world's greatest modern art has been made by British artists.

In this book we will look at some of the most famous British artists of the last few decades and find out where their art can be seen.

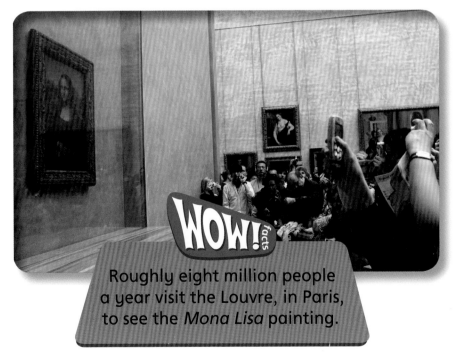

WOW! facts

Roughly eight million people a year visit the Louvre, in Paris, to see the *Mona Lisa* painting.

2. ANTONY GORMLEY

Many people may not be able to spot the artist Antony Gormley from a crowd but his work is world famous and often on a very large scale.

He is probably best known in Britain for his large sculpture in Gateshead, Newcastle Upon Tyne, called *The Angel of the North*.

At first, many local people were against it and thought it spoilt the landscape. That all changed when a stunt was unveiled – one of Newcastle's most famous footballer's shirts had been made specially to fit the sculpture! The people of Newcastle loved it and, although the shirt didn't stay on for long, the people's love of the sculpture still remains.

WOW! facts

The Angel of the North is 20 metres tall and is over 50 metres wide.

Almost all of Gormley's work is based on the human body. He often uses casts taken from his own body to make the pieces. The figures are made from materials that can withstand being outside in all weathers.

In 1998, a work called *Another Place* was installed at Crosby Beach, near Liverpool. Gormley's figures stand in different places up and down the beach, looking out at the horizon. The sea even comes in around some of the figures and they can be seen standing out of the sea. Again, like *The Angel of the North*, many of these figures were dressed up by local people and the public grew to love the artwork on show.

Gormley later made many more of these figures and took them on a tour around the world, placing them in famous cities, such as London and New York. The work was called *Event Horizon* and many people would walk around the cities trying to find the figures. Some were on the streets but others were on top of buildings and hidden from the main walkways.

He won the Turner Prize in 1994 with *Field for the British Isles*. This artwork was made up of 40,000 small, handmade figures. This work has also been moved around and it was even displayed in a church.

WOW! facts

Antony Gormley was knighted in 2014 for all the work he does in the the art world. He is now called Sir Antony Gormley.

3. ANISH KAPOOR

Anish Kapoor is an Indian-born British sculptor. He is another artist who likes to work on a very large scale. One of his most famous sculptures, *Cloud Gate*, can be seen in Chicago.

It is possible to walk right up to it and touch it. He wanted his art to blend into the city's landscape. By using a reflective surface, he could show the people of Chicago the wonderful and interesting landscape that they already had around them.

Kapoor often works with very bright colours. He was inspired to use such bright colours by the many colours of spices he saw in India.

He designed the *ArcelorMittal Orbit*, which is at the
Olympic Park in East London. The tower, as well as
being a piece of art, was used as a viewing platform
during the London 2012 Olympic Games and there is
now a restaurant at the top.

One of Kapoor's largest works was housed at Tate Modern in London. *Marsyas* took up the huge Turbine Hall, stretching all the way from one end to the other.

In 2006, he created a piece of art called *Sky Mirror*, which was exhibited at the Rockefeller Center in New York.

Like Antony Gormley, Kapoor has also received a knighthood.

4. DAVID HOCKNEY

David Hockney makes his art in many different ways. He is a painter, stage designer and photographer, among other things. In the 1960s, he was involved in the 'Pop Art' movement, which included many famous artists, such as Roy Lichtenstein, Peter Blake and Andy Warhol.

He was voted by fellow artists as the most important British artist of the 20th century. Hockney has made many works of art, but some of his most interesting work involved him taking hundreds of photographs and then joining them up to create a scene. He called these 'joiners'.

He discovered this method of working by accident. He did not like photographers using cameras with wide-angle lenses and he used to take many Polaroid photos of his home and stick them together. As he looked at his photos that were stuck together, he thought they looked like they were telling a story of movement, as if the viewer were walking around in the scene.

What do you think?

5. RACHEL WHITEREAD

Rachel Whiteread is one of Britain's most famous female artists. She creates sculptures that are usually casts of objects and spaces.

One of her most famous works was called *House*.

The piece was a large cast of the inside of a house. The cast was made from concrete and it showed the empty space that could be found in an average family home. She exhibited it on the exact spot in London on which the house had originally stood. This piece won her the Turner Prize but the local council still knocked the sculpture down to make way for new homes.

Another one of her works, *Embankment*, filled the Turbine Hall of Tate Modern. This time, she had taken casts of the insides of cardboard boxes.

6. DAMIEN HIRST

Damien Hirst may be the most recognised British artist working today. He is known for making art that can be seen as shocking. He is Britain's richest living artist and is said to be worth £215 million. He was born in Bristol but grew up in Leeds. He did not do very well at school and was often in trouble. He saw art as a way of expressing himself.

For one of his most famous works he placed a four metre long dead shark in a glass tank and kept it in a liquid that stopped it from rotting.

He also did the same with other animals, such as sheep and cows.

WOW! facts

Damien Hirst has created works of art using a whole range of animals, including ducks, insects, fish and horses.

As well as using dead animals in his art, he has also painted. His famous 'spot paintings' were a collection of paintings that were completely made up of coloured spots. He didn't actually paint most of these – he would get his assistants to do them. They still sold for a lot of money!

Hirst is always trying to come up with new ways of surprising people and in 2008 he decided to sell a complete collection of his art called *Beautiful Inside My Head Forever*. It shocked the art world by selling for £111 million, breaking all records for an art sale.

He is also responsible for the world's most expensive piece of art, *For the Love of God*. It is a platinum cast of a human skull, covered with more than 8,000 diamonds, and has real human teeth. It is worth £50,000,000.

Like Anish Kapoor, Hirst also played a part in the London 2012 Olympic Games by creating a British Union Jack flag as a centrepiece in the closing ceremony.

7. POLLY MORGAN

Polly Morgan never thought of becoming an artist. She always wanted to be an actress but, after she took a course in taxidermy, she changed her mind.

She has since made many artworks that have appeared in shop window displays in London and galleries around the world.

The animals she uses in her work are given to her by vets and pet owners. All of the animals used either died naturally or in accidents, and she likes to keep a log of how all the animals died.

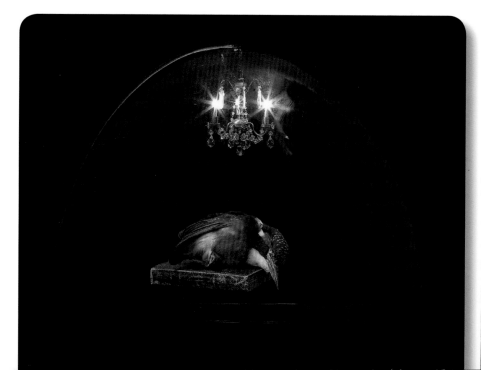

Questions and answers with Polly Morgan

Q – Why is art important?

Art is important for different reasons. It can make you feel calm or angry, safe or confused, and it can make you laugh or feel sad. I think of it as poetry that you can see.

Q – What do you enjoy most about being an artist?

Making art has the power to change my mood. I can hide away in my studio when I'm feeling upset or frustrated and always come out feeling better. I also enjoy the feeling that I can think something into existence! And no matter where I am, or what time of day it is, I can be working.

Q – Do you have a favourite piece and, if so, what is it and why?

My favourite artwork is usually whatever I'm making at that moment.

8. BANKSY

One of the most famous British artists is a street artist called Banksy. However, like many graffiti artists, he keeps his identity secret. If you search the internet, a few possible names come up but no one really knows who he is.

Banksy's work was first seen on walls in Bristol but later artworks started to appear in London and then all over the world. His art can appear suddenly overnight in any location.

His early work was usually made with spray paint and stencils, but he has also made sculptures and paintings. His work often highlights, and sometimes makes fun of, political and world issues. His images have been seen by millions of people around the world.

In 2013, he exhibited a new set of artworks around the streets of New York. One day he set up a stall with an old man selling real, original Banksy artwork. The artworks were worth up to £20,000 each but they were being sold for £38! Nobody knew it was real artwork by Banksy and the stall only took £263. The next day, the stunt was on every news channel in the world and only then did the lucky customers realise their artworks' true value!

Banksy has even managed to sneak works of art into galleries. Sometimes they hang there for days before anybody notices that they are there.

There are a lot of fakes made and it is often up to art experts to decide if it is really by Banksy or not. Real Banksy artwork is sold for millions of pounds and is seen as some of the most fashionable art to own.

Do you think this is the work of just one artist?

9. MODERN ART GALLERIES IN THE UK

Tate Modern

Tate Modern can be found next to the River Thames in London. It is the most visited modern art gallery in the world, with nearly five million visitors every year.

It was originally a power station, but it was converted into an art gallery and it opened in 2000. The most impressive section of the gallery is the Turbine Hall. It is five storeys high and displays one specially-made artwork there for around five months of each year.

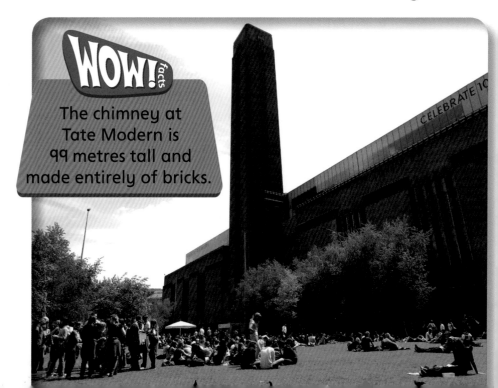

WOW! facts

The chimney at Tate Modern is 99 metres tall and made entirely of bricks.

Tate St Ives

Tate St Ives is located on the coast in Cornwall and was opened in 1993. It shows work by modern British artists. Also run by Tate St Ives is the Barbara Hepworth Museum and Sculpture Garden, which is nearby. Here, visitors can get up close to the many sculptures displayed in the garden of the studio where Barbara Hepworth used to live and work.

Yorkshire Sculpture Park

This open-air gallery is set in parkland and visitors can see sculptures by international and British artists, including Barbara Hepworth and Henry Moore.

This book shows just a small sample of modern British art and artworks. There are many more artists to discover and lots more artworks to explore around the UK. Have fun!

INDEX